T0195853

# THE
# VAV
## COLLECTION
### STOMP ON THE DEVIL'S HEAD

*Valerie Clay Brooks*

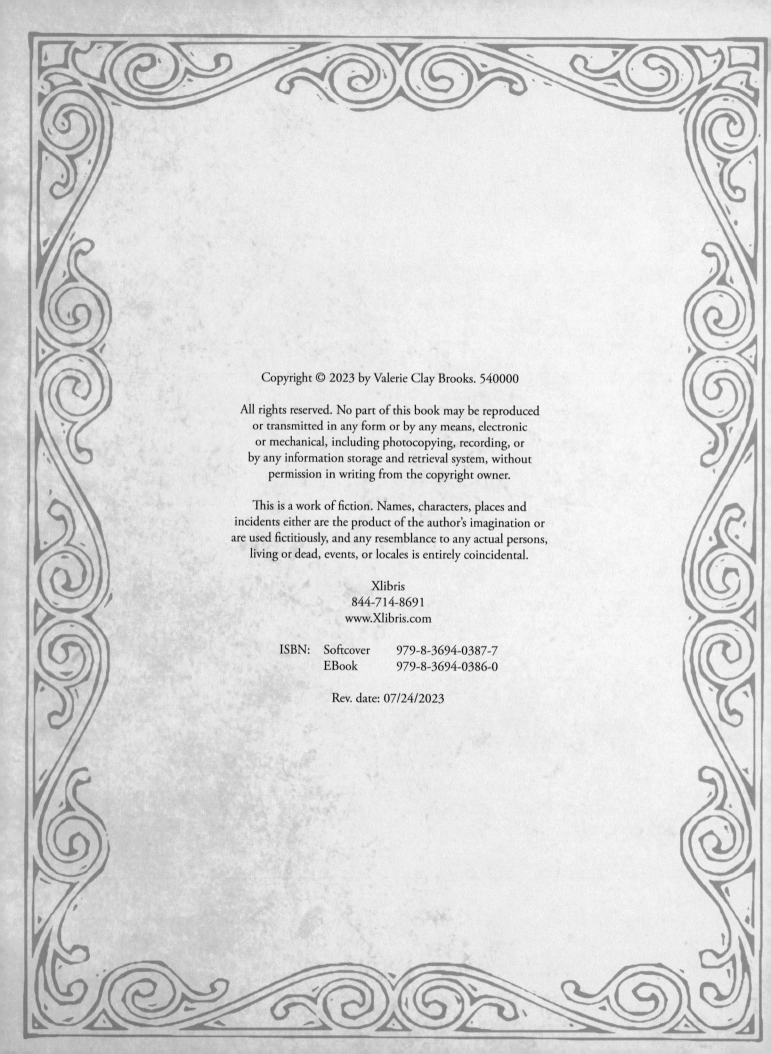

Xlibris
844-714-8691
www.Xlibris.com

ISBN:    Softcover        979-8-3694-0387-7
         EBook            979-8-3694-0386-0

Rev. date: 07/24/2023

# Contents

Come Into My Heart Lord.................................................................1

In the Presence of the Lord..............................................................3

Mirror, Mirror.................................................................................9

You Are My Friend.........................................................................11

Stomp On The Devil's Head............................................................13

Temptation....................................................................................19

Jesus You Are My All In All............................................................21

# Come Into My Heart Lord

Lord I will praise you all day and all night
Lord I need you to win this fight
The devil is trying to destroy me
I need you beside me to lead me
Come into my heart Lord. I'm letting you in.
Come into my heart Lord. And take care of me.
I know that you are the one who delivers
I know that you will deliver me
Come into my heart Lord. I've been lost for so long
Come into my heart Lord. I can't live on my own
I need you beside me. I know that you're here
I know that you will deliver me
Come into my heart Lord. I'm waiting on you
I know that you hear me. I know that you do
I will not worry. I know that you're here
I know that you'll deliver. I know that you will.
Come into my heart Lord. I've been lost for so long
Come into my heart Lord. I can't live on my own
I need you beside me. I know that you're here
I know that you will deliver me.
Lord I will praise you all day and all night
Lord I need you to win this fight
The devil is trying to destroy me
I need you beside me to lead me
I need you beside me to lead me
I need you beside me to lead me.

# In the Presence of the Lord

## (Feeling of Love)

I am in the presence of the Lord
I am in the presence of His Love
I am in the presence of the Lord
I am in the presence of His Love

It is a feeling that I cannot believe
It is a feeling that comforts me
It is a feeling of love

I am in the presence of the Lord
I am in the presence of His Love
I am in the presence of the Lord
I am in the presence of His Love

When I was fallen on the side of the road
It was Jesus that was my tow
He picked me up and He carried me
Oh Lord, it is a feeling that is hard to believe

For I am not worthy of His Kingdom
I am not worthy of His love
For I am not worthy of His Kingdom
I am not worthy of His Love

But my Lord, He thought differently
He picked me up, He said, "Girl come follow me"
For I will show you things you have never dreamed
A world of peace and love, which is everything

For I am not worthy of His Kingdom
I am not worthy of His love
For I am not worthy of His Kingdom
I am not worthy of His Love

Cont.

Peace and love my Father is
Peace and love my Father is
Peace and love my Father is
Peace and love my Father is

For I am not worthy of His Kingdom
I am not worthy of His love
For I am not worthy of His Kingdom
I am not worthy of His Love

I am in the presence of the Lord
I am in the presence of His Love
I am in the presence of the Lord
I am in the presence of His Love

It is a feeling that I cannot believe
It is a feeling that comforts me
It is a feeling of love
It is a feeling of love
It is a feeling of love
It is a feeling of love

# Mirror, Mirror

Mirror, Mirror on the wall who do you reflect today?
Mirror, Mirror on the wall who do you reflect today?
What will I see when I look, when I look into your gaze
Will I see the face of my Lord, or will I see something unkind
If I do not see the face of my Lord, I know I got to work on me

Mirror, mirror on the wall who do you reflect today?
If I do not see the face of my Lord, I know I have got to get down and pray
I have got to say, "Lord please help me to become the way you want me to be."
If you do not see your love shining through me, then Lord please help me

Mirror, mirror on the wall who do you reflect today?
All I want is others to see how your love shines down on me
I want them to see how great you are so they too will get down and pray
I want them to rise and worship you because you are worthy every day.

Mirror, mirror on the wall who do you reflect today?
Lord I just want you to know, I love you in every way.
Lord I just want you to know, I love you in every way.
Lord I just want you to know, I love you in every way.

# You Are My Friend

Jesus Christ is the one for me.
I will be waiting for His return
He will come and take me home with Him
I will be waiting for Him. He is my friend.
He is a friend to all who will let Him in.
He says, "Come and be with me."

So if you want to feel His Love within,
Then accept Jesus Christ as your friend.
He died for all of us so that we may live again.
Now, tell me that, that is not a friend.

Jesus, Jesus you are my friend.
Jesus, Jesus I am accepting you in
Jesus, Jesus you are my friend
Jesus I accept you in. (twice)

Jesus Christ is the one for me.
I will be waiting for His return
He will come and take me home with Him
I will be waiting for Him. He is my friend.
He is a friend to all who will let Him in.
He says, "Come and be with me."

So if you want to feel His Love within,
Then accept Jesus Christ as your friend.
He died for all of us so that we may live again.
Now, tell me that, that is not a friend.

Jesus, Jesus you are my friend.
Jesus, Jesus I am accepting you in
Jesus, Jesus you are my friend
Jesus I accept you in. (twice)

# Stomp On The Devil's Head

Stomp on the devils head, do not let him into your life.
Stomp on the devils head, do not let him into your life.
Stomp on the devils head, do not let him into your life.
Stomp on the devils head, do not let him into your life.

Depression and fear and insecurity
Rebuke it in the name of Jesus, my dear.
Sickness and disease, do not let it take it over your life.
Call on God and win that fight
Foolishness, drug addiction, do not let it control your thoughts
Call on God and win it all.

Stomp on the devils head. Stomp, stomp on the devils head.
Stomp on the devils head. Stomp, stomp on the devils head.

Jump up and down, and spin around
Just praise the Lord, and take the devil down
When you believe in God, you will believe in yourself
Stomp on the devils head and better yourself.

Stomp on the devils head. Stomp, stomp on the devils head.
Stomp on the devils head. Stomp, stomp on the devils head.

Release all of your anger
Release all of your doubt
Release all of your worries
And your fear, take it away

Stomp on the devils head. Stomp, stomp on the devils head.
Stomp on the devils head. Stomp, stomp on the devils head.

Stop all of your lying. Stop all of your running around
Promiscuity will wipe you out

Cont.

Stomp on the devils head. Stomp, stomp on the devils head.
Stomp on the devils head. Stomp, stomp on the devils head.
Stomp on the devils head. Do not let him into your life
Stomp on the devils head. Do not let him into your life


Depression and fear and insecurity
Rebuke it in the name of Jesus, my dear.
Sickness and disease, do not let it take it over your life.
Call on God and win that fight
Foolishness, drug addiction, do not let it control your thoughts
Call on God and win it all.

Stomp on the devils head, do not let him into your life.
Stomp on the devils head, do not let him into your life.
Stomp on the devils head, do not let him into your life.
Stomp on the devils head, do not let him into your life.

# Temptation

It was always around me temptation
It was always around me, I see.
It was always around me temptation
It was always lurking after me

Get away from around me temptation
Do not come around here bothering me
Get away from around me temptation
My Father will see to thee

I will call out to Jesus in Heaven
He will come after you in a flash
Get away from me temptation
Cause you are a thing of my past

I have given my life to Jesus
And you cannot steal that from me
My Lord will protect me forever
Because my Lord is good to me

You see I have decided to follow
His word to the "T"
And as a result of my following
He continually blesses me

I won't trade that for any foolishness
That no longer exist within me
So flee from me around me temptation
My Lord said to tell you to flee

(You have been rebuked in the name of Jesus)

# Jesus You Are My All In All

LA, LA, LA, LA, LA, LA
LA, LA, LA, LA

LA, LA, LA, LA, LA, LA
LA, LA, LA, LA

Jesus you are my all in all
Without you I would not be here

Jesus you are my all in all
Without you I could not live

Your grace and mercy has saved me
All I can do is praise you

I praise you Lord
I praise your Holy name
I praise you Lord
I praise your Holy name

Jesus you are my all in all
Without you I would not be here

Jesus you are my all in all
Without you I could not live

With you I can claim the victory
Over all of my enemies

With you I can claim the victory
Because I know my savior lives

Jesus you are my all in all
Without you I would not be here

Jesus you are my all in all
Without you I could not live

LA, LA, LA, LA, LA, LA
LA, LA, LA, LA

LA, LA, LA, LA, LA, LA
LA, LA, LA, LA

Printed in the United States
by Baker & Taylor Publisher Services